Read Along Rhymes

These rhyming stories help to make early reading an exciting, enjoyable shared experience for children, parents and teachers. They are designed to be read by adult and child together, or by children in pairs. The 'join-in' or 'read along' text is contained in speech bubbles, giving children an active role in the story-telling. The pictures and speech bubbles together give the outline of the story – the full story is told in the verse below. *Read Along Rhymes* can be used in conjunction with any reading programme.

The stories can be used flexibly, as perfect 'take-home books', linking home and school. They can also be used by teachers as part of their language programme, matching a book to a child, and developing the content within each book.

Read Along Stories

If you've enjoyed *Read Along Rhymes* you will be sure to get a lot of fun out of *Read Along Stories* (25 titles).

1   The Hungry Snake
2   Fresh Fish on Friday
3   The Mischievous Monkey
4   Gilbert the Goat
5   Hen Looks for a House
6   The Clever Worm
7   The Robber Rat
8   Dirty Dan
9   Mr Tubb's Tap
10 The Witch's Ball
11 Ant's Apple
12 Nails for Newt
13 Cat's Cake
14 The Little Indian
15 The Strange Umbrella
16 The Envious Elephant
17 An Orange for the Baby
18 The Magic Vase
19 The Two Wizards
20 The King who Couldn't Kick
21 The Queen who Wouldn't be Quiet
22 Snakes and Ladders
23 Yawn Yawn Yawn
24 A Jumper for Grumper
25 Peter's Pink Panda

Suggestions to parents

It's a good idea to try and find a quiet place to sit together, away from distractions. First look through the pictures together, stop and talk about what's happening in the story: what's in the pictures, how the characters are feeling, what's going to happen next, and so on. You can have fun with the repetitions, the exclamations and the rollicking rhythms of the verse.

The Great Jam Robbery

It was boiling hot that summer day
When Pidding people went down to the bay.
It was the afternoon of the carnival race.
There was no-one left in the whole of the place.

Except for Sam, he was ill in bed,
His head was hot and he looked all red.
He sat at the window and watched them go
With buckets and spades and rafts in tow.

The carnival race was lots of fun.
The rafts were launched, some weighed a ton.
They'd plenty there to eat and drink.
Which raft would win and which would sink?

They all got wet, the grannies snoozed,
The children splashed, the ice-cream oozed.
And everyone there had a wonderful day,
That afternoon at Pidding Bay

And not until the sun went down
Did people start back home for town.
'But what is this? It's very queer,
Some dreadful crime has happened here.'

For all the doors stood open wide.
The people screamed and rushed inside.
'There's been a thief. Is something taken?'
They all looked white and very shaken.

'We must discover all that's gone.
Just look in here, there's something wrong.'
From every kitchen shelf in town
The jars of jam had been taken down.

For there on all the kitchen tables,
Stood empty jars with just their labels.
Poor Mrs Hedge had lost a dozen,
She'd saved them all to give her cousin.

At least another hundred more
Lay empty in the Co-op store.
Of all this raspberry, peach and plum
Not a jar was left, not a single one.

Just think, whoever could consume
Twelve hundred jars in an afternoon?
Who could have done it? Where is Sam?
Perhaps he knows who ate the jam?

They found young Sam was out of bed.
He was holding up a book he'd read.
'Look here it is, plain as can be,
That dinosaur! It winked at me!

It was really huge, it broke the doors,
It grabbed the jars between its paws.'
'The poor boy's mad. He's got the flu.
It's just a tale. It can't be true.'

They heard a shout from down the street.
It was Joe from the factory, white as a sheet.
'Just look at these great footprints here!
It's not a dog, that's very clear.'

And there just by the factory door
Were jam prints made by a giant claw.
'So there you see, it's true,' said Sam,
'A dinosaur did eat the jam!'

The people cried, 'What shall we do?
The dinosaur might eat us too!'
'There isn't any chance of that.
It's just a Sauropod in fact.

The book says here, their teeth are weak.
They live on plants, they're pretty meek.
These footprints lead right out of town.
Let's see if we can track it down.'

The grownups came, the children too,
The keeper from the local zoo,
The police and fire brigade and mayor,
The whole of Pidding Town was there.

'Just follow me, come on,' said Sam,
'I'll show you who ate all the jam.'
The tracks led up beyond the hill.
There lay the beast! It looked quite ill.

'Stand back,' said Sam, 'it's very sick.'
The keeper said, 'We must be quick.
Its teeth I think are really bad.
You'd better let me help you, lad.'

The dinosaur gave such a groan,
Some people turned and fled for home.
'This comes from eating too much jam.
You'd better stick to plants,' said Sam.

The keeper tugged, Sam held its jaw.
A tooth came out. 'There's still one more.'
Just one more tug. At last it's out.
The crowd began to clap and shout.

'Oh look!' they cried and some went pale.
The beast stood up and wagged its tail.
Some eighty tons the huge thing weighed.
'Don't eat us please!' the people prayed.

But all it did was give a wave
And set off homewards to its cave.
'I think it's had enough of jam.
It won't come back again,' said Sam.

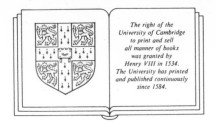

*The right of the
University of Cambridge
to print and sell
all manner of books
was granted by
Henry VIII in 1534.
The University has printed
and published continuously
since 1584.*

Published by the Press Syndicate of the University of Cambridge
The Pitt Building, Trumpington Street, Cambridge CB2 1RP
32 East 57th Street, New York, NY 10022, USA
10 Stamford Road, Oakleigh, Melbourne 3166, Australia

First Published 1989

Printed in Hong Kong by Wing King Tong

British Library cataloguing in publication data
Potter, Tessa
  The great jam robbery
  1. English language. Readers – For children
  I. Title II. Vyvyan-Jones, Marc III. Series
  428.6

ISBN 0 521 35495 1 hard covers
ISBN 0 521 35760 8 paperback

DS